COMING OUT: COMING INTO GRACE

by

CANDACE M. RESPRESS

PROLOGUE

My friend,

I am writing this to you not just to tell you my story, but in hopes that through my story, you will understand the great redemption that lies in the hope of the one true love. I could go right into telling you of this love, but I need to you understand the process through which redemption comes. There are two parts to this redemption process that I will speak of to you: the first part is my coming out. I am going to be uncomfortably transparent with you. There are aspects of my life that you may or may not know; however, for you to understand my love and why I am so in love, I must be honest about the events through which I have lived.

My hope is that you will not see this as a judgment. Truly, I am not judging anyone; I write this with the sincerest love that is in my heart. There are things that I did not understand in the past that are much clearer to me now. My heart cries out to share this knowledge with you of a love that everyone can have, if only it is received.

If at any point I embarrass you, I apologize; that is not my intent. Truly, I love you. Otherwise, I would not pour myself out like this, but please know that I want more for you than even I have. If I make you uncomfortable, well, that is going to happen. No one can grow without experiencing a little discomfort. When children grow, their appetites increase so much that it seems that they can just never get enough. Even teething babies are irritated by the changes that take place inside their mouths. Despite the discomfort, they are delighted by the new sensations of the food they can now experience because of this alteration. I humbly ask that you bear with me through this process, because there will be growing pains, but the satisfaction of the experiences you will have after are well worth it.

The second part of the process of redemption is coming into grace. This part is especially difficult for those of us who pride ourselves on being independent or self-sufficient. It is much easier for us to give gifts than it is for us to receive them. We work hard for and try to earn everything that we get; yet this grace is something that no one can earn, but must be willingly received to come into redemption. Grace is free and unmerited favor. Favor is an act of kindness beyond what is due or usual. My hope is that when you hear my story, you, too, will receive this grace. Like me, you will find the greatest love that you will ever know: the one true love.... and so begins my story.

CHAPTER ONE

A s I tell you my story, keep in mind that it does not necessarily fit the stereotypical environment for which people think these situations generally occur. I point this out to remind you that we will never know what everyone encounters in life, nor can we justify a situation based on environment or culture. We make a bad habit of saying that things happen because "they grew up in a single-family home," or "Mom was this and Dad was that," but those generalizations do not fit everyone.

I grew up in a home where both parents were present. Not only were both parents present, but both of my parents were also college-educated; they both held white-collar, federal jobs. They both were also active members of a local Baptist church. My family was by no means rich, but I never suffered want. As young couples often do, my parents had to make a decision about childcare. Any parent who has had to make this decision knows that daycare is expensive, especially in the summer months. I am not sure about the particulars of how the arrangement came to fruition, but one of my aunts stayed with my family that summer. Since she was staying, she watched my older brother and I while my parents were at work; I was four and my brother was seven.

I don't remember much about that summer, but a few things do stand out. I remember that Michael Jackson's album, *Off the Wall*, had been out for almost a year. It was my aunt's favorite record; she was, and still is, a huge Michael Jackson fan. I remember this because music was a constant in my home. From Sesame Street's *C is for Cookie* to the Commodores to Stevie Wonder, there was always music playing. Of course where there is music, there is singing and dancing. We would belt out songs at the top of our lungs with my mama, and there was always a spot on Daddy's dance card for me.

I remember playing outside with my older brother and the boy across the street. We played football, basketball, and baseball. The rules were often altered for this little girl, until they figured out that I was athletic. Then, in the middle of a game, they would change the rules back to the real rules to ensure that they did not lose to a little girl. There were many games played, but the most significant game was the one that my aunt played with my brother and I.

This game was not like the rest of our summer games; this was a secret game. The rules of this game were different for each child. For me, it went like this: imagine playing hide-and-seek, and no one ever coming to find you. That was how the game began for me. I would hide, but no one would look for me. I would find myself, at four years old, locked out of rooms, all alone in a big, two-story house. I would knock on the door, but I was told that I could not come in because I wasn't old enough to play.

"What do you mean I'm not old enough to play? I want to play. Why can't I play? What are you doing in there? And why did you stop playing with me?"

I am still amazed at how easily someone can be drawn into whatever is going on by simply excluding him/her from the beginning. That is how I was drawn into this game of fondling and touching. We touched my aunt in "special" places to show her how much we loved her. She touched us to show us how good it felt and how much our "favorite" aunt loved us; it was our secret.

Forget that secret stuff! We told! We snitched! We went straight to our parents and told them that we had been touched inappropriately! They kicked her out, sent us to therapy, and everyone lived happily ever after. I wish that were true, but my parents would have no idea that any of those things happened for the next twenty-six years. We kept the secret bottled up and repressed. We knew that if a stranger were to touch us in our private places that we were to tell our parents as soon as we could; however, this was unchartered territory. This was a family member, and a female family member at that. Families did not discuss protocol for when you were touched by an aunt; at least, my family didn't. Besides, we were playing a game, right?

Now, I know what you are thinking: "Candace, that is horrible. How could she do that to you?" Don't go making me a victim just yet; I am just informing you of what happened so that you will understand later in this story where Satan started working his plan in my life.

I do want to interject for just a moment. This is very important: I hold no ill will toward my aunt because of the past. I have forgiven her. You may wonder how I could forgive someone who could molest children. Honestly, un-forgiveness kept me trapped and bound to the molestation. Un-forgiveness kept the wound open for the enemy to wreak havoc in my life. There is a reason that God says vengeance belongs to Him, *Romans 12:29, KJV.* He knows that un-forgiveness is like drinking poison and expecting the other person to die. He knows that un-forgiveness is like sitting in a prison cell with the door wide open, but never walking out of the cell to freedom.

I tell you this because we must forgive to move forward: without forgiveness, I left the door open for anger, rage, depression, low self-esteem, bitterness, rejection, and abandonment. I laid the foundation and built the framework for sexual sins of all natures, including, but not limited to, homosexuality.

Homosexuality is a sin. That may be hard to swallow, but in all truth, it is a sin. For some of you, you may wonder why you have felt this way your entire life. From a small child, you can probably remember having feelings for, and attraction toward, members of the same sex. That does not make you a freak or a weirdo; it just means that Satan has placed a design on your life that needs to be separated from you. It means that as a small child, or even as a baby in the womb, Satan used some event to place a design that, if acted upon, places a curse on your life.

You may wonder what a design is: for me, it was molestation; for some, it is rejection in the form of an absentee or over-critical parent; for others, it is a parent that really wanted a girl instead of a boy, or a boy instead of a girl. It is a seed planted by Satan that if properly watered, will grow. A design is Satan's plan to get you away from God's will.

The really cool part is that the curse can be broken; there is always a way back to God. It comes through surrender, but we will get to that in a bit. Let's look at what the design looked like in my life.

CHAPTER TWO

I f you have not already figured it out, I am going to talk about homosexuality. I am not going to just talk about it in the context of sin, even though it is a sin. Rather, I want to talk about it in the context of Christ and the freedom He brings from all sin. Don't worry; homosexuality is not the only sin I will discuss. There is a swarm of sin that circulates around this particular sin that is not limited to the person involved in homosexuality.

For every action, there is a consequence. Some consequences are blessings based on actions, inside of the will of God. Other consequences are curses based on actions outside of the will of God. For me, the consequence of the game played with my aunt was from the age of five years old forward, I was attracted to girls. The strange part was that I was also attracted to boys; however, my attraction to girls seemed so much more significant because that did not fit with anything that was supposed to be natural. Even at the age of five, before I had been taught anything about the laws of attraction, I innately knew this was something to keep hidden.

I could name a different girl every year from kindergarten until my college years that I had a crush on that I never openly admitted. I also had boys that I had crushes on that outside of shyness I had no trouble admitting. I grew up in the south. I was an active member of a local Baptist church. Attraction to the same sex was not something that was talked about without someone thinking the worst possible things about you. Homosexuality was like the cooties: if you got too close to someone with it, you would catch it. So, I never mentioned those feelings. Like everyone else, I had boyfriends. Most of my boyfriends circulated around my involvement with sports. I was a bit of an athlete. Some would say tomboy; I would say athlete who did not like to wear dresses. These boys were really friends that I spent a great deal of time with, due to common interests. Most of the girls that I was attracted to had a different kind of femininity that I did not feel I possessed. I was attracted to boys that were like me and girls that were the opposite of me. In my mind, it did not really matter, because I would never tell anyone the way I felt about girls and I would never act on it, or so I thought. Then I went to college.

College was a rough time for me; I lost a lot of mental and emotional security in college. I almost completely lost myself in college. I never realized how many safety nets were in place for me until those safety nets were no longer there. I had an amazing support system in my parents. They were actively involved in almost every aspect of my life: coaching me in softball; teaching me in Sunday School; shuttling me back and forth to choir practice, Girl Scouts, basketball practice, track, church play practice, youth department trips, band. They were there. My church was also very present in my life. Although I did not always appreciate the wisdom that was given, there was always someone imparting wisdom into my young mind. That all seemed to vanish when I went to college; everything that I thought I knew now seemed very different, as I developed a new family of complete strangers with very different values than mine. I was lost: I wasn't smart enough, good enough, pretty enough. Boys were only interested in long hair, and there were plenty of girls telling me that I was on the "other team"; I just did not know it yet.

Looking back, the breakdown in my wall of security was astounding. I went from someone who would never be with a woman, because it was wrong, to someone who had a ton of questions as to what made you gay. I dated guys here and there, but none of them were interested in any sort of relationship. The one who was interested moved to another state for a job. Neither one of us felt a long-distance relationship would work, so that was that. With that, Satan's plan really took flight. I had already been rejected, and now I was abandoned to seal the deal.

In the fall of my senior year, I became good friends with a freshman on my softball team. It was awesome because my best friend was in love, and I did not really see her anymore. Most of the friends that I hung out with had graduated, and I was pretty lonely; but in this teammate, I had a new friend.

Life was okay again. I must have seemed down because this girl made it a top priority to cheer me up. Anytime I was not in a great mood, she was there to put a smile on my face. We were friends.

One night, we went out to eat with two other teammates; dinner was fun. We came back to the dorm having a huge giggle fest. Satan set the trap, and I took the bait. That giggle fest turned into "What have I done?" That "What have I done" turned into the norm for my life. All the hidden feelings that I had held onto came rushing back to the surface. This was love; I am a Christian. I know that I've accepted Christ as my Savior, so maybe everyone else is wrong. The deception was complete.

CHAPTER THREE

I t is amazing how our emotions can change the way we behave and think; our feelings can easily sway us. Even more frightening is how sex makes us lose all sense of logic and reasoning. It makes us forget everything we hold to be morally true. Sex is a dangerous weapon in the hands of the enemy.

In the time after my first relationship with a woman, I was very confused. I was not open about that relationship, and I definitely was not looking to "come out". In all honesty, I was not sure it was something that I would ever put myself through again. I was not prepared for the emotional damage that a break-up brings, and I had no one that I could discuss it with because I had pretended that it didn't happen. I felt lost and betrayed; I had no idea who I was, or what I had become. At one point, I decided that I would go back to dating men, but something had been ignited in me: something that I began to crave; something that would not easily go away. An identity began to form, based on the happenings of my life. This identity was not who I truly was, but this identity protected me from hurt and kept me from the rejection that I'd come to hate so much.

My friend, many of whom were my former teammates, were trying to help me figure out who and what I was, so they did what they thought would be most helpful to me: they invited me to the gay bar. It was a very awkward experience for me to begin with, but soon it became part of my routine. I would go country line-dancing and two-stepping on Thursdays, and then go clubbing on Saturdays. Saturdays made a lot more sense in the scheme of things than Thursdays did because I hated country music, but it was a way for me to meet girls. I was very shy when it came to trying to make a romantic connection. The easiest way to make connections was for me to learn to dance to country music and let them pick me up. I did not know what to say, but I could dance; it worked for me. As I began to go out more and more, I began to conform to a lifestyle that felt natural. In this setting, I didn't have to hide; I didn't have to pretend; I could just be. I began to incorporate myself into this lifestyle. I would go to gay bookstores, support gay-owned restaurants, play in the gay softball league, and, of course, annually attend the gay pride festivities: all the while searching for that one who would love me that I could love back.

The more I conformed, the more I changed. I began to take on the mannerisms of the women that seemed to always have someone interested. I began to dress more masculine; that was not too much of a stretch for me. I was always athletic. I had been a tomboy my entire life. Men's clothing always seemed more comfortable to me, and I was never trying to show off my curves. I even began to change my personality. I had always been a very sweet person, which helped me make lots of friends, but never a girlfriend. I started using cheesy pick-up lines and carried myself with an air of arrogance. I did many jerkish things that seemed to pique the interests of the attention I'd been trying to attract. My friends began to openly say that I was different, but I really did not care because girls were flocking to me. I was not lonely anymore, or so I thought.

Now, I'm not going to tell you that during this time I stopped believing in God; that would be a lie. I still considered myself a Christian. I still believed that Jesus Christ came in the form of man, lived a perfect sinless life, died on the cross for all my sins, and rose again on the third day. I had accepted Christ as my savior at the age of seven. Regardless of the way I was living, I still held my belief to be true. Many of my friends did not have the conversation with me about Christ, because they knew where I stood. We fundamentally had different theological beliefs: I believed that Jesus Christ was my Savior; they had a hard time believing in God at all.

I occasionally went to church. I would have this longing to be in the house of the Lord to worship, not realizing that my spirit man was crying out. I had dry bones and did not realize it. I was longing for a relationship, but I was looking for it in the wrong places; I became a walking contradiction. I started talking to one woman, who, for some reason, decided that I would be a better fit with her friend. This new woman stimulated me intellectually, and a relationship began. During this time, I decided to go back to school to become a teacher, so we moved. In this new city, I made a point to find a church. I wanted her to go with me, so I searched for a church that was gay-friendly. I was in a monogamous relationship, and I wanted us to serve God together. I believed that if I died, I would go to Heaven, but because she was agnostic, she would go to hell. I did not want her to go to hell, so I tried to convince her to go with me.

I even found a gay-friendly church that would be accepting of our lifestyles; in other words, I found a church that would tell me about the love of Jesus Christ, but not tell me that my sin was sin. If we are truly honest with ourselves, that is what most of us do: we search for truth; we search for meaning; we look to do and be right. We even look for and expect others to do and be right, but we never want to be corrected when we are wrong. Instead, we look for those who will validate everything that we want as okay. Some people call it political correctness, conformity. Sometimes political correctness is conformity, but at times, anti-political correctness is also conformity.

I eventually changed churches, partially because my girlfriend stopped going with me, but the other reason was that I was not growing spiritually. The church was politically-charged and not Christ-centered. It was ritualistic and not biblical. The new church was a little church that provided me with sound biblical doctrine. Did that change the fact that I was living a homosexual lifestyle? Of course not; I was convinced that I was good. That is because my focus was getting and staying in the gates of Heaven, not on a relationship with Christ. I had no idea that I was missing the most important aspect of anyone's life: a relationship with Christ.

CHAPTER FOUR

T he relationship with that woman ended, and a new relationship ensued very shortly thereafter. Unlike any other girlfriend I'd had, this woman was also a Christian. She also believed that Jesus came to save the world and died on the cross for our sins. She had accepted Christ as her Savior at a very young age, much like me. She grew up in church with her family having active roles in the church and youth department. She understood my beliefs. She wasn't trying to get me to choose between her and God; she felt that she needed to get back to her roots and go back to church.

I finished my teaching degree and got a job in another part of the state. We moved with an agenda: start a new life in this new town, start building careers, and find a church home. We were set on being a little family that would pray and worship together. We believed that in recommitting our lives to Christ, He would bless our lives as a family. We were going to live according to biblical principles, except for that part about homosexuality. Like many Christians, we believed that not everything in the Old Testament was applicable to modern-day today. To truly understand that rationale, all you need to do is look at the many sins that are present in the church today and see why it would be easy to get tripped up.

There are scores of single people living in fornication by having sex outside of wedlock. People look at having sex and living together before marriage as a pre-requisite to marriage. There are some churches that still say it is wrong, but so many churches just turn their heads. Part of the reason for that is many ministers are in the pulpit proclaiming the Word of God, but are secretly, or not secretly, engaging in adulterous relationships. Everyone knows because gossip is also running rampant in churches. While we're honestly discussing sins in the church, you also have the people who believe they have perfected the lie. They will look you straight in the eye and lie to you, while simultaneously placing curses on their own and on family members' lives. We just decided to live our private life, privately. There was no need to discuss what went on behind closed doors; it wasn't anyone else's business. If you asked, we might tell you if we thought you would be accepting, but just like we were not going to get into your business, there was no need for you to be in ours. With that, we became active tithing members of a local non-denominational church. We did not go openly as a couple, but as really good friends and roommates.

The interesting part was that we began to grow; that is truly a demonstration of how much God loves us. Even though we were living a lifestyle of sin, He did not waste a thing. The more we went to church, the more we grew. The funny thing about growth is that it always brings discomfort in some form. When you grow physically, your clothes become uncomfortable because they do not fit anymore. You remain uncomfortable until you buy new clothes that fit. The same thing happens when you grow spiritually in Christ. Those old sinful clothes don't fit anymore, so you become uncomfortable. Now, I don't know anyone who, when their physical clothes didn't fit anymore, choose to keep wearing the clothes that they had outgrown. That is why I don't understand why when we outgrow our old spiritual clothes, we continue to hold on to them. We refuse to let go of that one thing that would set us free by releasing it.

As we grew spiritually, we each came face to face with our sexualities. It never happened at the same time: there were times when she would question and pull back, and other times it was me doing the questioning. With the choice to not face what God was asking, we chose to turn our backs to God in that area, leaving ourselves open to attacks by Satan; and attack he did. We struggled financially. We probably did not struggle as much as we should have because we were faithfully tithing. We were simultaneously placing blessings and curses on our lives. At times, we struggled for our sanity; relationship paranoia caused us to believe the other was leaving or seeking someone else. We each began to constantly question the other's loyalty and do hurtful things in return. I cannot speak for her, but rejection, anger, rage, and

depression began to change me even more. I was in self-pres-
ervation mode, and the enemy had a plan to take my life.
Of course by this time, we were no longer going to church
on a consistent basis and moving further from Christ. My
main concern became my relationship and my finances; when
faced with the choice, I chose the old clothes.

CHAPTER FIVE

S omeone who is controlling and overbearing dictates your every move and expects you to follow those rules; a tyrant forces your hand. God is neither controlling nor is He a tyrant. If He were, so many of us would not have gone through the things that we have gone through. Instead, we would have lived perfect lives, whether or not that was our desire, and hated Him because of it. However, because He is a loving God, He gives us the choice. Sometimes our choices manifest into bad things for others or ourselves. We generally blame God for allowing those things to happen, but if He did not allow them to happen, He would not truly love us, and He would be the tyrant that He is so often labeled.

God allowed my choice to not draw near, as He called me closer to Him and away from my lifestyle. In doing so, He allowed all hell to break loose in my life; infidelity, manipulation, alcoholic tendencies, uncontrolled financial accountability, and abuse from both sides began to take place. There were many times that I wanted it to all end, regardless of how that happened; I didn't want to be here.

I drove by this particular church every day on my way to work. I'd glanced over a couple of times, but didn't even know how to get there. You could see the church from the main road, but the entrance was on another road. One Sunday, after not going to church for a couple of months, I decided to go back to church. Instead of going to my old church, I felt the need to make an abrupt turn down a different road, as I was passing the church that I saw every day going to work. As I turned, the road curved around, and I was soon pulling into the driveway of the church from the road. I walked through the doors and was greeted with, "Welcome to the Kingdom". Those very words set off sparks in my spirit.

The thing that I love about my church is it is a church that will tell you the truth, but does so in love. Is it a perfect representation of Christ? Of course not; no church is. It is made up of imperfect people that are just like you and me. The difference is that these imperfect people pray and believe in their prayers. These imperfect people read their Bibles and try to live according to that Word. These imperfect people seek God, while striving to live more like Christ. When they fall, they get up and keep pressing to reach that mark. This church, full of imperfect people, taught me about a relationship with Christ. It is the Body of Christ, fit with all of the scars that He carried following His resurrection.

In the beginning, I had a hard time getting over myself, and the many things that I knew made me imperfect, so I ran. I ran because they loved me. They had no idea who or what they were loving: I was broken; I was lost; I was so undeserving, but they loved me anyway. They would see me out in town walking into a bar, or with a drink in hand. They never accused, but instead would tell me how good it was to see me, or that they missed me. They would love me.

When I would take a break for an extended period of time, they would call me just to tell me they loved me and to see how I was doing. Never a "Where have you been?" Only a "How are you doing?" They even loved me when I came in smelling like a bar from the night before. They didn't crinkle their noses, but hugged me full on with extended arms of love.

I know what you're thinking: "That would be great if all churches just showed unconditional love." Yes, that is what my church did for me, but they also told me truth. They showed me how sin kept me bound. Sin made me a slave to that very sin I was committing. They showed me that unless I truly repented of my sin, I could not be free. My pastor is never one to pull a punch. When he preaches, he tells the truth, according to the Word of God. He tells the truth to the marriages about what the Bible says a husband's responsibility is to his wife and a wife's responsibility is to her husband. He tells singles the truth about celibacy and keeping ourselves until marriage. He tells us about our identities in Christ, and how homosexuality is an attack on those very identities as God created us. He does not accuse; he only says what the Word of God says. *John 1:1, (KJV)* says, "In the beginning was the Word and the Word was with God and the Word was God." *First John 4:16b, (KJV)* says, "God is love, and he that dwelleth in love dwelleth in God and God in him." If God is the Word and God is love, then how can anyone separate the two of them?

Too many times, the world tries to separate the two to justify the desires of their hearts. Fornication or sex out of wedlock is justified by love. Adultery is justified by love. Homosexuality is justified by love. There are so many things that are justified by love, but if they go against the Word of God, they cannot truly be love because He is both. He is His Word, and He is love. This is a hard truth for people to accept; it was hard for me to accept. I could always understand that Jesus loved me enough to die for my sin. I had the faith to believe that He was resurrected three days after His death, conquering sin and death. He was my Savior, but I discovered He was not my Lord. This revelation came as the relationship that I clung to so desperately ended. I really had two choices:

blame God or trust God. This time, I chose to trust God and try things His way.

CHAPTER SIX

I am truly amazed at the grace and mercy that Jesus Christ shows each of us. The years that followed that last relationship are what I refer to as "the process". I call it a process because, in the time since that break-up, Christ has been, and still is, transforming me into His original design. Like a skilled gardener, He is pruning away things that can no longer remain attached to me. Like a master sculptor, He is chipping away pieces of my past that are not a part of His finished product. Sometimes this process is very painful. There are times that those that I hold very dear to me don't understand what God is doing to me. They don't understand the changes that God is making. They sometimes take offense, not understanding that there is a picture that is so much bigger than me.

I have become a vessel that the Lord is using to bring all of His children to Him.

There are certain things about my past that made it difficult for me to move closer to God. Going out was one of those things; there was a group of people that I knew from several different places. They knew me as Candace who is a lesbian, and not as Candace who is a child of God. In most places that I went, there was a label attached to me. In order for me to not be attached to that label, I stopped going to places that recognized that label as my identity. I really did not have a choice. Every time I went out, I got sucked back into that identity. No one understood that I was trying to live according to God's will. The temptation was often too much for me; when I went out, I would fall. Then I would feel guilty and ashamed. I would take my sins to the altar on Sunday, but I was still stuck in my sin. I would cry. I would beg. I was trying so hard, and I was failing.

I did not understand God's grace. The amazing part of God's grace is that you don't have to do; you just have to be. I know that does not make sense. The world tells you that you must do this right; you must do that right. If you don't do everything right, you are bad; you are condemned. Grace says to just be and receive. Grace says that there is a supplier who will give me everything that I need. I have but to receive what He is giving and be who He created me to be. You may wonder what this grace is; it is very simple. "God demonstrates His own love toward us, in that while we were yet sinners, Messiah died for us" (*Rom. 5:8, TLV*).

One of the most difficult things for me to understand has always been God's love for me; in a logical sense, His love does not make sense to me. I look at my flaws and my past mistakes, and I feel inadequate and undeserving. When I look at the list of my flaws, I see liar, homosexual, fornicator, adulterer, pride-filled, and lover of pleasure. Please believe me when I tell you that I could keep going, but that would be depressing. However, when He looks at me, He sees daughter; not just any daughter, but chosen and beloved daughter. I know it sounds crazy, but it is very simple. When I chose His Son, He called me daughter. When I chose His ways, He called me His chosen daughter.

I am going to remind you: I chose His Son long before I chose His ways. There is a common misconception that we must have everything together before we can come to Christ; that is simply not true. Romans 5:8, which is His Word, tells you that is not true. You hear people say "Turn your life around and come to Christ." I have a radical thought for you, friend: how about instead of you turning your life around and then coming to Christ, come to Christ and give your life to Him so that He can turn your life around? Just to be clear; I'm going to step it out for you:

STEP ONE: Come to Christ. This includes all of your messes: every negative thought, action, and deed that you, or anyone else, can think of you are coming with you to Christ. You are bringing Him all of your dirt, hidden and unhidden.

STEP TWO: Give your life to Christ. This requires making an intentional choice in submitting to His will for your life, and relinquishing control of your destiny to Him. You must also accept the free gift of salvation that He gives for no reason other than His love for you.

STEP THREE: Allow Him to turn your life around; this must come after Step Two. Since you are no longer in control of your life, but have given it to Him, He is now able to freely reign in your life and fulfill His will for your life. He will begin to show you your purpose, as you move closer to Him in relationship.

It is relationship with Him that makes Jesus Christ and His way so different from any other religion. Without this relationship, I would still be lost to my sin. Without this relationship, I could never know the greatest love my heart will ever know: the love of a Father displayed by His Son, manifested inside of me by His Spirit.

CHAPTER SEVEN

I desperately want you to understand that God loves you. I believe so many times, people speak for God and say that He hates the sinner instead of Him hating the sin. If you are homosexual, bisexual, transgendered or confused, God does not hate you: He does hate the sinful acts that you commit. He does hate that you've lost the identity that He gave you, but He loves you. He desires to be in relationship with you. He has a desire that all of His creation would turn back to Him. He does not want to lose a single one, but He is true to His Word and His law. He gives us the choice to accept Him or reject Him. Remember, while we were yet sinners; while we were still doing our dirt; while we were doing our messes and enjoying doing it, He died.

That is such an amazing love story to me. Over two thousand years ago, Christ loved me so much that He took all of my sins, past, present, and future, along with all of humanity's sins for all time, on the cross and died. He literally died for me. I look at the selfish, self-serving things that I've done in my lifetime. I look at the wrong, deliberately sinful, and manipulative things that I've done. I don't deserve anything from Him, but He loves me anyway. He gave me a chance for restoration. He gave me a chance for transformation. He gave me a relationship like I've never experienced before. He gave me His grace.

The great news is that grace is not just for me; it is for you, too. Jesus Christ wants to be in an intimate relationship with you. The really cool part is that it does not matter what you have done in your life. You could be a murderer or just tell a few white lies. Your sin does not have to stand in the way. It is really very simple; you only have to confess with your mouth that you are a sinner and that you need Jesus to be Lord over your life. You have to believe in your heart that He is true to His Word; that Jesus rose from the dead, and you will be saved.

It is a free gift to accept. Regardless of your sin, He offers you life. To man, there are big sins and little sins; but to God, there is only sin. He offers freedom for all of His creation. You can be free; just call on the name of Jesus. His grace will supply all of your needs.

If that is your choice, share your wonderful news with someone. Become a part of a church family. If that church family is not willing to give you both love and truth, it is not the church home for you. Be prayerful about your decision. God will lead you to the place that will help you grow in His will and walk in your purpose. If you are not ready to make that choice just yet, remember, God loves you so much that He leaves His offer on the table until the day you die. That is true love; that is my true love.

I pray that His peace brings you comfort; that your heart is filled with His joy; that He fills your mind with understanding; and that you are surrounded by His love. Be blessed, my friend.

With all my love,

Candace

ACKNOWLEDGMENTS

I am truly thankful to my Lord and Savior, Jesus Christ. His vision truly amazes me; that He would use me. I don't know. His thoughts are higher than mine, so I'll just trust Him. I thank Him for the people that He has blessed and surrounded me with in this process. I am thankful for my prayer and accountability partner Misti, who has been there to pray for me, give me encouraging, truthful words, and talk me through this whole writing thing. Thanks, sis. I am thankful for my three wonderful editors: Carrie, Leslyn, and Sara, who provided me with great feedback and the extra little push that I needed. I am thankful for my pastors and spiritual parents of the flock, Apostle and First Lady Goode, for the anointed teaching that they give our entire KCI family.

I am thankful for my entire KCI family; your love and support are immeasurable.

I am thankful for my wonderful brothers; my fierce protectors who stand by me no matter what. I know you sometimes think that I'm crazy, but you love me. I am also so very thankful for my biological and my first spiritual parents, BR and VR. I am learning that it is not a common thing to have parents that are spiritually sound in the Lord. My parents set a foundation that I know was key in bringing me back to the Lord. For you, I am extremely grateful that you were obedient to the call of parents to train up your children in the Lord and discipline with the rod of correction. Thank you for loving me.

CPSIA information can be obtained
at www.ICGtesting.com
Printed in the USA
LVOW10s0219220417
531768LV00011B/72/P